Lesson from the two Dad

Learning valuable financial intelligence for better success

By

Roy Black

Table of content

Introduction

Get yourself truly prepared financially. What did your people show you about life, money, and finding a calling? Did they tell you to go to class, truly center in, and find a nice profession a brief time later? No doubt. Actually, nonetheless, that isn't exactly phenomenal admonishment, yet it is all that most gatekeepers tell their youngsters, and most educators too Goodness, while we're examining school, here's another request for you: while you were there, what did you learn about acquiring cash? If it was out about acquiring cash? If it was a house they can manage, and they focus on taking care of the home loan. They own their vehicles for quite a long time and keep away from vehicle installments; however, they might purchase a pre-owned luxury vehicle and keep it running for a very long time. They are satisfied with what they have while they construct their organizations and portfolios. Furthermore, they bring in their cash sincerely. There is a common misconception that most moguls are liars and cheaters. One falsehood is that the wealthy don't cover their assessments; however, the best 1% pay 40% of the duties. Another falsehood is that the rich are unscrupulous con artists and that they just got affluent by harming others. As a general rule, studies show that the main characteristic of tycoons that they consider key to progress is honesty. You can't remain in business assuming you're known for defrauding clients or being sued for extortion constantly. Nor could you at any point make the quality connections that are important to fabricate a business organization assuming you're a liar

Chapter 1

Rich people don't work for cash,and the unfortunate mentality

What is the distinction between a rich and unfortunate mentality? How does the effective contrast with most of us? Such countless individuals don't acquire independence from the rat race since they don't have a certain something: the right outlook. Everything begins with your opinion on cash, riches, and achievement. It's anything but an issue of karma, birth, or associations.

The greatest contrasts among rich and needy individuals can be traced back to attitude, standpoint, and conduct. The rich and the poor contrast not just in the amount of money they possess but also in the way they think.

Rich individuals have a perspective that is not quite the same as that of poor and working-class individuals.

They ponder cash, abundance, themselves, others, and life. Thus, you will have a few elective convictions from which to choose. Along these lines, you can discover yourself thinking as needy individuals do and immediately switch over to rich individuals' thought processes.

An inspirational perspective, zeroing in on making the best decision, ignoring greatness, turning into a ceaseless student, and taking a cautious gamble are contrasts between the rich and poor. This lessens their chances of becoming poor after calamity strikes, and it assists them with accomplishing their monetary objectives over the long haul.

A rich outlook will advise you to be independent and construct various surges of pay. It will advise you to form a group of more brilliant individuals than you and use the endeavors of gifted individuals. The mentality of the rich is the most definitive justification for why "the rich continue to get more extravagant, while the poor get less fortunate. Bill Entryways has been cited as saying, "In the event that we weren't actually employing extraordinary individuals and pushing ahead at maximum speed, it could not be difficult to fall behind and turn into some average organization. Anyway, which outlook do you have? We should look at twelve frightening contrasts between how rich individuals think and how poor or working-class individuals think.

Rich outlooks grasp the worth of schooling.

Unfortunate outlooks are unmindful of the significance of steady learning or education. Rich attitudes help people acquire and refresh their abilities throughout their lives.

Schooling remains a significant determinant of lifetime pay. Note that this doesn't mean

you need to go to a costly, confidential school or acquire a postgraduate education. Notwithstanding, you almost ensure that you'll be poor in the event that you don't complete secondary school.

One contrast between the rich and the unfortunate is that the rich figure out the worth of information. They're not part of the 40% of adults who don't read a book subsequent to graduating high school. They're perusing industry distributions to get familiar with their field and succeed at work.

They're finding out about cash management and self-improvement with the goal of improving throughout everyday life. They're continually learning. They'll guarantee that they keep up their accreditations, and they'll proactively acquire extra certificates to fit the bill for raises and advancements.

Rich mentalities are better in danger. The executives

Unfortunate mentalities frequently lead to anxiety about facing new challenges. The rich aren't betting with their cash, whether it is going on outings to the club or facing huge challenges with penny stocks. They are mindful so as to oversee risk. One way they do this is by having the right protection and inclusion. They have life coverage, health care coverage, and handicap protection with the goal that an individual fiasco doesn't clear them or their families out. They won't simply begin a business or speculation without examining its benefits.

They have crisis assets with a lot of reserve funds, so they can cover a significant startling cost without venturing into the red. They focus on safeguarding themselves rather than burning through cash on things they care about. This doesn't mean they don't put resources into stocks or land. It implies they get their work done before putting away cash.

They research the properties and the expenses to recover them and sell them before they purchase them. They research stocks or common assets prior to putting in their cash. Instructing themselves about different subjects lessens their gambling level. Also, to that end, one of the distinctions between the rich and unfortunate outlook is that the poor frequently live in apprehension about fiascos, while the rich hope to have the option to face the hardship.

Rich individuals fabricate different floods of money.

Destitute individuals have one source of income: their work.

Destitute individuals set up their assets in one place by being subject to one stream of pay.

The affluent are known for their hard-working attitude; however, there are a lot of individuals who try sincerely yet stay in need. There are multiple ways that the rich work in unexpected ways. One is that they commit time to arranging their monetary future. They put something aside for retirement so they have a separate stream of income before they need to resign from their work.

They forcefully pay down obligations and try not to assume new obligations, so their pay goes further. They commit time to taking care of their ventures while managing their money each month, whether it is in a 401K or investment properties. In the event that they own a business, they benefit from it to produce extra pay.

It very well may be permitting protected innovation or leasing one of the suites to produce extra income. They might hold normal everyday employment except to educate or counsel as an afterthought to procure extra pay. This can be a type of chance administration, as well, since it gives them an early advantage if they lose their employment or basically need to begin their own full-time business.

Rich Outlooks Have Confidence in Saving, Money Management, and Duplicating

Unfortunate outlooks go overboard with materialistic things.

Needy individuals wind up saving nothing to contribute.

Rich outlooks save, save, save. They save 10% to 20% of their net gain consistently. The rich are deliberate. They don't put something aside for what's to come. They begin saving with each check, and they decide not to go a little overboard so they can make that next 15% commitment to retirement.

They don't say they'll take care of the obligation later. They make an arrangement to settle obligations and follow it for many months until they're without obligations. As per "The Mogul Nearby" and Chris Hogan's subsequent book "Regular Tycoons", most tycoons by total assets either follow a spending plan or intentionally send a set rate to investment funds and live off the rest.

To put it plainly, they devise designs and follow them. They put forth objectives, and by zeroing in on them and continually pursuing them, they regularly accomplish them. Note that it isn't simply cash. This is also the reason the affluent are less inclined to be overweight. Assuming you're now used to reliably pursuing monetary objectives, an activity and diet plan is only another arrangement to follow. Keep in mind that for anybody to go too far from destitution to riches, they need to have a significantly different mentality. If you have any desire to get rich, then you want to really change your attitude and start to see things from the viewpoint of the well-off.

Instructions to conquer a troublesome season of money

Troublesome financial times can prompt feelings of stress. The following are ten methods for facilitating your uneasiness by zeroing in on the region of your life over which you have control.

Cash stresses can set off pressure in individuals, everything being equal. Watch for indications of stress in yourself and in your loved ones. These may include changes in resting or eating patterns, cerebral pains, peevishness, outrage, trouble concentrating, and sorrow. Assuming you are experiencing issues with pressure, deal with yourself by eating right, getting sufficient rest, saving normal time for exercises you appreciate, and learning ways of unwinding. In the event that you can't deal with the weight all alone, look for help from an expert. Your medical services supplier can help. You'll likewise track down numerous supportive assets on this site for monitoring pressure.

Arrange with loved ones for everyday reassurance and offer thoughts regarding cash-saving tips.

Help each other through this season of monetary vulnerability, both by offering everyday reassurance and by pooling your assets. You could, for instance, carpool together, shop at bargain retailers together to set aside cash, or even share the expense of kid care.

Survey your financial plan and cut pointless costs. Track your spending and trim the additional items, like takeout feasts, digital TV, or diversion. Save at the supermarket by utilizing coupons and purchasing more affordable brands. Assuming you have any cash left over, utilize the reserve funds to pay off obligations and assemble a secret stash. Monetary specialists prescribe saving sufficient cash to cover three and a half years worth of everyday costs. That might have felt overpowering to ponder a little while ago; however, begin with limited quantities today and make it a more drawn-out long-term objective.

Work on diminishing your obligations as much as could reasonably be expected. This will help you feel less stressed overall. You'll find numerous supportive assets on this site on ways to pay off past commitments.

Work with lenders on the off chance that you are in the red.

Call every lender and request more modest, regularly scheduled installments, diminished financing costs, and an additional opportunity to take care of your obligation. Most lenders will attempt to work with you in the event that you make sense of your circumstances and exhibit that you mean to meet your commitments by paying even a limited amount every month. Make certain to know precisely what you can bear before you call your leasers. You would rather not focus on something you will not have the option to finish.

Survey your retirement and reserve fund plans with an expert. Try not to settle on momentary close-to-home choices with long-haul money growth strategies. Meet with a trusted monetary consultant prior to pursuing any choices to offer resources or move cash to various records. In the event that you don't have a monetary consultant or organizer, ensure you pick one who is guaranteed with the Confirmed Monetary Organizer Leading Group of Guidelines.

Chat with your supervisor, assuming the circumstance is influencing your work or efficiency.

Assuming that you are working longer hours, are stressed over work vulnerability, are encountering sensations of stress or overburden, or are managing different issues at work, talk with your administrator about your interests and about potential arrangements. Additionally, center your work around ways of lessening your pressure. Throughout your break, practice 5 minutes of profound breathing activities or escape your work area for a short walk. Both are great ways of decreasing pressure. Recall how you've confronted troublesome difficulties before. What worked for you, then? How might you utilize a portion of those procedures now? Just helping yourself to remember your abilities can assist you in feeling more in charge of the ongoing circumstances.

Make it a point to look for help.

Your representative help program (EAP) can assist with a scope of issues connected with funds and stress. Contact the program for data and assets. Exploit assets to assist with seeing you through troublesome monetary times. In the event that you are experiencing difficulty meeting lodging, food, utility, clinical, or other bills, get in touch with us for additional help. If you regard your course like this, you'll go through your entire time on earth pulverizing your soul to extend your pay, while others—the public power, bill finders, and your managers—take most of the honor. As of now, lots of people really follow the sad of their mantra, but many do it in view of a sensation of fear, an overwhelming difficult situation at dismissing the suspicions that society drills into us. A stable job prompts wealth, we're told, so we center around it as youngsters and work extensively and more energetically as adults. The result? We may be avoiding desperation, yet we're emphatically not becoming any more affluent. Yet, there are sure to be people who don't educate their youngsters on that mantra—people who realize how money is made, extended, and stayed aware of. Rich people, in that capacity—people like Mike's father, the rich dad who transformed into a money-related coach to both young fellows So what did Mike's dad suggest? At every turn, nothing He made a plan with the young Kiyosaki, proposing to show him that he had some consciousness of money if the youngster would work for him at the meager speed of a dime an hour. Some agreed, but following a portion of a month of missing the mark, the youngster returned to his "rich" father, raging with shock and ready to stop. "You've exploited me enough," he said, "and you haven't even remained consistent with your responsibility. You showed me nothing in cash in such a long time! Be that as it may, it was not too far off: his most significant model, conveyed by his new guide with a slight grin. Some have, as of late, found that life habitually pushes them around. Additionally, he'd found that working for cash doesn't make you rich. Which is the explanation? Rich people don't work for cash. So you could ask yourself: if the well-off don't work for cash, then, at that point, how might they get prosperous? Through burglary, maybe, or by winning the lotto?

Chapter 2

Show yourself reserves, perceive authentic assets, and put assets into them.

Monetary assets are the data sources we use to create labor and products. Monetary assets can be partitioned into four classes: work, land or regular assets, capital, and business ventures (innovative capacity). Work alludes to human exertion and ability. Regular assets are things like land, oil, and water. Capital alludes to man-made gear like apparatus, structures, or PCs. At long last, a business venture includes the work and expertise to put a wide range of various assets together.

Imagine a pizza eatery. The financial assets expected to deliver pizzas include land for the eatery building and parking area, work to make and serve the pizzas, capital for the stoves, coolers, and other hardware, and a business venture to deal with the business and market the café. Without these assets, the pizza café couldn't exist as a business.

Monetary assets are fundamental for the functioning of any economy, as they are the data sources used to create labor and products that fulfill individuals' needs. The accessibility and proficient utilization of assets can fundamentally affect monetary development, work, and expectations for everyday comforts.

One of the fundamental motivations behind why financial assets are significant is that they are restricted in supply, which brings about the idea of shortage. Since there are insufficient assets to create every one of the labor and products that individuals need, social orders should pursue decisions about how to designate their assets. These decisions include compromises, as involving assets for one reason implies that they can't be utilized for another reason. The effective utilization of financial assets is, consequently, fundamental for boosting the results of labor and products and guaranteeing that they are circulated in a way that benefits society in general.

Example: Find out about this article.

Could we answer that request from the last book? No, it's none of the reactions above.

The rich become rich by having their money work for them. As opposed to consuming the sum of their compensation on ornaments and luxuries, they put a piece of it in assets of various sorts. What's more, thereafter, rather than working for cash, they let their assets acquire cash for them.

Regardless, we shouldn't forget about the central concern: when we left off, Robert was as yet a youth, and "asset" didn't have a spot in his language. Anyway, Mike's dad, the rich dad, planned to change all that.

On one occasion, he put the young fellows down and cleared up for them that the rich buy assets, but the less well off buy liabilities, habitually in the stirred-up conviction that it's actually assets they're getting. In truth, he got a handle on the fact that an asset is anything that adds money to your wallet. An obligation, on the other hand, is something that eliminates cash. This partition is crucial, and a moderately few people hit the bullseye. So we ought to look at a model.

A house is, as a rule, contemplated as an asset, right? Be that as it may, it's maybe the most serious gamble you can take. Buying a house regularly suggests functioning for as far back as you can remember to take care of a 30-year back home credit and neighborhood charges, meaning it eliminates cash from your wallet.

A house bought with home credit kills you in two ways: First, you're guaranteed to have an enormous expense diminish your compensation reliably for the accompanying 360 months, and this means that it's a gamble. Second, those 360 portions could have been placed into far more advantageous assets that put cash in your wallet.

Rich dad communicated the model as essentially as he could for the two young fellows: "In the event that you should be rich, you ought to just recognize certifiable assets and get them. Go through your lifespan buying liabilities, in any case, and you will not at any point make it."

Rich Dad checked out that a penniless person's remuneration goes directly to taking care of brief expenses like rent, obligations, and food. A common person's paycheck needs to take care of similar expenses too, as liabilities can include a home advance, school credits, visas, and various sorts of commitments.

However, rich people As opposed to requiring remuneration, their assets get adequate money to oblige them, and every now and again, you give them enough to contribute again—like stocks, securities, or land you rent to tenants. The eventual outcome of that re-hypothesis is that their compensation goes up once more, inferring that the rich keep on getting more extreme.

Yet again, this is so critical that I will say it: If you can keep your liabilities and costs low, you'll have the choice to put what's left over in assets and have your money work for you.

Do that, and soon you'll end up saving a little fortune.

Chapter 3

Avoid others' issues: acquire cash for yourself, not your chief

Regardless of how incredible a relationship you have with your chief, it's, for the most part, not the smartest plan to be companions with them.

That is on the grounds that an individual relationship can make things convoluted when they might have to settle on hard decisions, says Phoebe Gavin, an initiative and work environment mentor.

"According to by the day's end, assuming your manager's supervisor says, 'Hello, we can't stand to utilize your companion any longer. You really want to lay them off; do you understand what your manager will do? [They're going to lay you off," Gavin tells CNBC Make It. "They could cry on the Zoom call with you, yet they sure will give you that formal notice."

This might appear to be cruel, but it's simply business, which she makes sense of. Pioneers in the work environment are responsible for results, including your exhibition and the presentations of others. Hierarchical fellowships can cause these outcomes to appear one-sided, and numerous American specialists concur.

Three out of five U.S. That's what representatives trust, somewhat; laborers who are companions with their supervisors get unique treatment compared with the people who keep things generally proficient, as per a 2015 Spherion study distributed on Franchise.com. Of those representatives, 56% say those laborers certainly stand out, and 52% say they get more adaptable timetables.

Past possibly setting off allegations of preference, supervisor representative kinships are inclined toward creating problems, Gavin adds. Ultimately, there will be a point at which those two intentions clash," she says. "Where their craving to do a good job for you will struggle with their obligation to their work,

To keep away from the "ponderousness" that might come from this, choose to "foster a warm, heartfelt relationship with your chief rather than becoming best pals, she says. This begins by breaking down your organization's culture and defining proper limits with yourself and your manager. Ask yourself, 'What is the way of life of this organization? Also, what is the way of life of the business?' And afterward, you need to check in with yourself," Gavin says. "Since every other person is relaxed and discussing how they got squandered toward the end of the week, you don't need to do that."

Your relationship with your boss ought to be founded exclusively on you taking care of your business, "not how well your characters gel together," she adds.

Gavin uses a cupcake as an illustration of what these communications ought to resemble.

"The cake is, do you go about your business competently? The icing on the cake is, do you for the most part cooperate so that it feels OK with one another and you can sort of exchange energy? What's more, the sprinkles say, "Gracious, my golly, I'm getting hitched."'

Example: to find out about your relationship and individual interests

At this stage, you should dissent. Definitely, censuring secure, "worthless lifestyle" occupations while encouraging people to acquire assets—yet how should you remain to buy those assets if you don't have some work anyway? Is the money expected to tumble from the sky?

No way. No one's encouraging you to stop your typical, ordinary work—not yet, regardless. What Kiyosaki stresses in his third model is the meaning of "avoiding others' undertakings".

By and by, that doesn't mean keeping your nose out of others' lives—not in this one-of-a-kind situation. It basically suggests watching out for your own assets and acquiring cash in like manner for yourself, in addition to your chief. In that capacity, avoiding others' undertakings suggests getting cash through your plan of assets rather than through headway, rewards, and raises.

With respect to individual spending plans, nonetheless, there's a differentiation between your calling and your business: Your calling is anything that you complete for 40 hours of the week to deal with the bills, buy food, and cover other everyday costs. Commonly, it gives you a specific title, for instance, "restaurant owner" or "leader". Your business, of course, is what you put time and money into to help foster your assets. With everything taken into account, how does this relate to Robert's movement toward money-related accomplishments? For sure, when he was young, his lamentable dad urged him to focus on finding a safeguarded and well-paying position. His rich dad, of course, encouraged him to start buying as Exactly when Robert was back in school, one of his main stories was the account of Robin Hood and his band of blissful men—the pack of journeying vagabonds who took from the rich to accommodate needy individuals. It was a thrilling story, he thought, but his rich dad clashed. All things considered, Robin Hood had all the earmarks of being a convict.

Rich's dad blamed the Robin Hood dream for propelling the obligation system he disdained. Also, as Robin Hood took cash from the rich and gave it to needy individuals, so too did the public power endeavor to take from the rich to accommodate the destitute.

Chapter 4

An enormous portion of us aren't given financial guidance.

Most Americans aren't conversant in the language of cash. However, we're supposed to settle on huge monetary choices as soon as our children are born. Would it be advisable for me to take on a large number of understudy obligations? Would it be a good idea for me to purchase a vehicle?—despite the fact that the majority of us got no proper guidance on monetary issues until it was past the point of no return.

While no course in individual accounting might have kept numerous Americans from becoming involved with the lodging bubble, obviously the vast majority of us need some assistance, ideally beginning when we're still in school. Also, I'm not simply looking at figuring out how to adjust your checkbook.

It's comprehension ideas like the time value of cash, chance and prize, and, indeed, the significance of investment funds.

This brings up the issue: What's all going on inside our study halls? Furthermore, what number of schools even suggest the subject? For reasons unknown, for a country that prizes moral obligation, we're doing very little.

"We really want to show the rudiments of financial matters and funds so individuals can settle on monetary choices in an impactful world," said Annamaria Lusardi, a financial aspects teacher at Dartmouth School and an exploration partner at the Public Department of Financial Exploration. "It's the accumulation of interest, the issue of expansion. These are the standards. What's more, these are truly logical subjects."

Research shows that this kind of monetary training will, in general, resonate with the understudies later.

Michael S. Drain, an associate teacher of family monetary administration at the College of Florida, concentrated on the issue in 2009 after he reviewed 15,700 understudies at 15 colleges who came from states with various (or nonexistent) individual budget tutoring prerequisites. The review was funded by the Public Blessing for Monetary Training, a charitable association in Denver that provides monetary education programs.

"Undergrads who came from states where there was a course required were bound to have a spending plan, were bound to be saving, were less inclined to have maximized their Visas somewhat recently, and were bound to be taking care of their charge cards completely," Teacher Drain said. However, his exploration likewise proposed that "social learning is extremely strong also," he said. "Everything that your folks say to you matters."

Guardians can help, yet many don't have the foggiest idea about the responses. Truth be told, some portion of the test is that numerous instructors don't by the same token. "We ought to foster a public norm for educator preparation," said Ted Beck, CEO of the blessing, which as of late led a review that tracked down that 64% of kindergarten through twelfth grade instructors (in states with monetary training rules) detailed feeling "not capable" to show those principles.

The norms generally alluded to were created by the Kickoff Alliance for Individual Monetary Education, which gives diagrams of a suggested individual budget educational plan. The points cover everything from pay and vocations to credit and obligations, reserve funds, contributing to gambling with the executives, and protection. Numerous teachers and monetary education specialists concur that savvy, extensive course materials now exist (you can track down an example in the web-based form of this story). The test is conveying them to study halls, and afterward uplifting states to order that it's instructed. What's more, preferably, it would begin significantly earlier than secondary school.

"It's hard in light of the fact that there could be no silver bullet to get this into each school," said Matthew Yale, vice president of staff to Training Secretary Arne Duncan. "It's not so straightforward as saying, 'We will establish this in the 100,000 government-funded schools in America.' Yet our arrangement for reauthorization accounts for monetary proficiency in schools, which is a huge, serious deal." Mr. Yale was alluding to the Obama organization's arrangement to update the Rudimentary and Optional

Training Act, ordinarily known as No Youngster Abandoned.

He said the Division of Instruction's subsequent stage is to work with locales and educators and assist them with finding the cash they need, whether it's through the numerous proficiency-disapproved charities or the confidential area. Mr. Yale additionally said that division authorities were dealing with cutthroat award programs, which would permit schools to vie for cash to pay for the monetary proficiency programs. As a joint effort with the Depository Division, the Training Office is right now running the Public Monetary Capacity Challenge, a web-based test for secondary school understudies that measures monetary skill and perceives remarkable entertainers, to assist with bringing issues to light.

President Bramble made the main Warning Chamber on Monetary Education in 2008, and President Obama plans to gather his own group. In its yearly report, the main gathering suggested that Congress or state governing bodies command monetary training in all schools for understudies in kindergarten through twelfth grade. Yet, will the new organization completely finish that proposal? Mr. Yale said training authorities were "not keen on presenting unfunded orders."

So what can really be done? As per Scott Truelove, who shows individual budget as a feature of a work-concentrate program for seniors at Chesterton Secondary School in Indiana, "It will take a parent's development.

They are the **central issue of this article.**

Okay, we ought to get back to the guidance story. At the point when you will get support from the induction for your own exchanges. They participated in his get-togethers with representatives, legal counselors, and accountants and found out what being a successful businessperson entails.

In this way, the young fellows gathered some valuable information, and they learned it quickly. Yet a little while later, they began to encounter issues. The capacities the pair were acquiring from their rich dad made it very hard for them to see school in a serious manner.

Over and over, they were educated that surveys and troublesome work lead regularly to advance and overflow; the likelihood that money-related instruction could moreover be critical didn't seem to happen to anyone other than a rich dad. Kids aren't taught about subjects like saving or monetary preparation, and as a result, they are oblivious to subjects like self-duplicate profits. Clear proof of this is the way that, today, even high schoolers every now and again amplify their charge cards. This shortfall in planning for money-related information is an issue for the current youth as well as significantly educated adults, a critical number of whom pursue lamentable decisions with their money. Think about it. A large number of individuals completely miss the mark on their retirement plans. In the US, half of the workforce is without benefits. Besides, of the rest, very nearly 75 to 80 percent lack advantages. Taking everything into account, clearly, society has left us ineffectually prepared concerning financial data. Notwithstanding, getting fiscally capable is one of Kiyosaki's key outlines. So what do you do? Teach yourself! Moreover, start spreading out a financial system.

Get yourself financial guidance by following

three phases: assess what's going on, set forth financial goals, and finally gather the money-related knowledge to reach them.

You can start the outing toward secretly putting cash away whenever in your life, but the sooner you get moving, the better. Obviously, if you start at 20, you will undoubtedly become more extravagant than if you start at 30.

However, regardless of your age, the best method for starting is by following these three phases. In any case, evaluate your assets. Second, set forth a couple of targets. Third, acquire the preparation vital to reaching them.

We ought to go through those in some more detail: In the underlying step, research your continuous money-related state. With your current work environment, what kind of pay might you at some point essentially expect now and later on, and what kind of expenses could you at any point financially manage? You could find that the new Mercedes you've been drooling over isn't sensible right now.

Remember: come clean! Furthermore, don't consider cash you don't have.

After this, you can advance sensible money-related targets. You could say that you accept that Mercedes ought to be inside in five years' time. Kiyosaki's soul mate Kim held up for quite some time, and over the long haul, she got her Mercedes from the benefits of their apartment buildings.

OK, the accompanying stage is to then start manufacturing your money-related knowledge. Contemplate this as an interest in the best asset that anybody could expect to find in you: your cerebrum. Sort out some way to oversee cash.

For example, if you're uncertain about exclusion, try working for a short time for an association that advances the cause. While you

Most likely, you will not get a shocking remuneration; you'll obtain a lot of capacities and confidence, which will be uncommonly useful later on.

You can, in like manner, further foster your cash tutoring. in your additional time. Pursue finance classes and courses, read books regarding the matter, and endeavor to organize with trained professionals. Did you get that? Yet again, could we repeat these methods: assess what's going on, set forth financial goals, and finally gather money-related understanding to reach them? If you base your money-related foundation on these construction blocks, there's a nice open door for you to turn out to be wealthy one day. Additionally, park that Mercedes in your garage.

Chapter 5

Money-related information and strength allow the rich to "compose" cash in any situation.

In this book, we will look at your disposition toward money-related issues. Since, assuming that you might want to change your continuous financial state, you'll need to start dealing with your assets.

The best change you no doubt need to make is figuring out how. In light of everything, if you don't defeat fear, you'll allow phenomenal entryways in life to pass you by. That is the explanation for why the persistent and the smart fight fiscally much of the time—their fear of society's disappointment holds them back from leaving a "vain lifestyle" and becoming rich. Moreover, their tension toward losing cash is a serious area of strength, which holds them back from placing assets into stocks or various assets. They disregard the worth of that accomplishment, which by and large takes guts.

That is the explanation for how financial understanding can be diminished to two key trimmings: data, clearly, and, what's more, mental determination. These two components set the rich apart from every other individual. Additionally, that is model 5.

Financial information allows the rich to "prepare" cash in any situation. They're prepared to perceive important entryways; they know how to respond to them; and they have the genuine pondering to own everything to the end. According to an outer viewpoint, it appears like they're essentially lucky, but believe it or not, they're making their own karma.

Taking part in Rich Dad's gatherings, Robert and Mike attended an outline school that couldn't teach them. In actuality, accomplishment takes guts, not just troublesome work. When you solidify your strength with financial data, you can perceive potential entryways quickly and gain from every one. Toward the day's end, you can almost "come up with" cash.

Chapter 6

As opposed to staying away from any pointless gamble, make a pass at placing your money in stocks, securities, or cost-liability securities.

OK, we ought to dig a bit deeper into chance in this book. What does it truly mean? Regardless of anything else, confronting difficulties suggests not constantly being counterbalanced and safeguarded with your money, which is what you're doing when you put it in fundamental checking and financial balances at the bank.

As opposed to playing it safe, have a go at placing your money in stocks or securities. While these are seen as more hazardous than normal records, they have the chance of creating significantly more wealth. Now and again, very much like with stocks, this can happen in an uncommonly short period of time.

Of course, if you would rather not surrender to the monetary trade, there are various endeavors that will help foster your overflow for a really long time. Take land or somewhere around there called charge line announcements. With charge lien confirmations, supporting costs range somewhere in the range of 8% and 30 percent—significantly higher than 0.21 percent, which was the commonplace ledger advance expense for America in 2013.

Clearly, the higher the potential for return, the higher the bet. With stocks, for example, there's reliably a slight open door where you could lose your entire endeavor. Nonetheless, if you don't confront the test regardless, you're guaranteed not to make any colossal returns.

So you see that facing those more noteworthy challenges and managing the more serious perils they present is essential to start making a more prominent compensation. It is what a rich dad would accept as what we ought to do. Advantages of Holding Money

There are most certainly a few advantages to holding cash. At a time when the stock market is in decline, holding cash assists you in keeping away from additional misfortunes. Regardless of whether the financial exchange rate drops on a specific day, there is generally the potential that it might have fallen or will fall tomorrow. This chance is known as a methodical gamble, and it tends to be totally avoided by holding cash.

Cash is additionally mentally mitigating. During upset times, you can see and contact it. Not at all like the quickly waning equilibrium in your money market fund, money will, in any case, be in your pocket or in your ledger in the first part of the day.

Notwithstanding, while at the same time moving to money could feel quite a bit better intellectually and assist you with keeping away from momentary financial exchange instability, being an insightful move over the long haul is improbable.

At the point when a misfortune isn't exactly a misfortune

At the point when your assets are put into stocks and the securities exchange goes down, you might feel like you've lost cash. However, you truly haven't. Right now, you've just caused a paper misfortune.

Be that as it may, assuming that you offer your property and move to cash, you are secure in your misfortunes. They go from being paper to being genuine. While paper misfortunes don't feel much better, long-haul financial backers acknowledge that the securities exchange rises and falls. Keeping up with your positions when the market is down is the main way that your portfolio will have an opportunity to benefit when the market bounces back.

A circle back in the market can put you right back on track to earn back the original investment and perhaps put a benefit in your pocket. Conversely, on the off chance that you sell out, there's no desire for recuperation.

Expansion is a money executioner.

While having cash in your grasp (or your portfolio) appears to be an extraordinary method for stemming your misfortunes, cash is no protection against expansion. Expansion is the rate at which the cost of labor and products rises. It's less sensational than an accident, but ultimately, the effect can similarly pulverize.

You might think your cash is protected when it's in real money; however, after some time, its worth disintegrates as expansion nibbles away at its buying influence. Obviously, expansion can affect profits over the long haul too. In any case, you can change your possessions and your portfolio's weightings towards developmentally arranged stocks. Interestingly, you can't do much with cash.

The Open Door Cost of Holding Money

The opportunity cost is the cost you pay to pursue a specific activity. Put another way, opportunity cost alludes to the advantages an individual, financial backer, or business passes up while picking one option over another.

On account of money, removing your cash from the financial exchange expects that you look at the development of your money portfolio, which will be negative over the long haul as expansion disintegrates your buying influence, against the likely gains in the financial exchange. By and large, the securities exchange has been the better bet.

Opportunity cost is the justification for why monetary guides advise against getting or pulling out assets from a 401(k), IRA, or another retirement investment vehicle. Regardless of whether you finally supplant the cash, you've lost the opportunity for it to develop while you contributed and for your profit to compound.

Be Cautious About Purchasing High and Selling Low

Presence of mind might be the best argument against moving money, and selling your stocks after the market tanks implies that you purchased high and are selling low. That would be the specific inverse of a decent money management system. While your impulses might be advising you to save what you have left, your senses are in direct opposition to the most fundamental principle of effective financial planning. An opportunity to sell was back when your speculations were in the haziest darkness, not when they were somewhere down and losing money.

At the point when you sell your stocks and put your cash in real money, chances are that you will ultimately reinvest in the financial exchange. The inquiry then becomes, "When would it be a good idea for you to take this action? Attempting to pick the perfect opportunity to get in or out of the financial exchange is alluded to as market timing. Assuming you couldn't effectively foresee the market's pinnacle and time to sell, it is profoundly impossible that you'll be any better at anticipating its base and purchasing it not long before it rises. The Reality You were glad to purchase when the cost was high since you anticipated that it would continue to climb perpetually. Now that it is low, you anticipate that it will fall for eternity. The two assumptions address mistaken thinking. The financial exchange seldom moves in an orderly fashion in either direction. Notwithstanding, generally, it has gone up. Indeed, living through slumps and bear markets can be nerve-wracking. Rather than selling out, a superior technique would be to rebalance your portfolio to compare with economic situations and standpoints, trying to keep up with your desired blend of resources. Putting resources into values ought to be a drawn-out process, and the drawn-out process favors the individuals who stay and contribute.

**Do whatever it takes, not just endeavor to
obtain; endeavoring to learn is extensively
more critical**.

As yet, we've found that your money should
work for you, we've learned about financial
understanding, and we've taken advantage of
serious areas of strength. In any case, there is
one more huge guide to acquire from a rich
dad. Right when Robert continued on from
school, he dealt with a reliable and well-
paying position rapidly. For a considerable
number of individuals, it would have been a
gift from paradise, and that is unequivocally
the manner in which his educated but
lamentable dad saw it. All things considered,
we certainly know it: the sad dad saw a Right
when Robert continued on from school, he
took care of a steady and well-paying
position rapidly. For a large number of
individuals, it would have been a little look at
paradise, and that is unequivocally the
manner in which his educated, sad dad saw it.

In other words, we certainly know it: the lamentable dad saw a strong job and constant work as the primary sure-fire technique for becoming rich. Not a rich dad, be that as it may, and not Robert at the same time. After around a half-year, he quit his work environment and joined the Marine Corps to figure out some way to fly. His awful dad was stunned, yet his rich dad commended him.

Why? Not because he enabled a lack of regard, but rather considering the way that he saw definitively the specific thing Robert was doing. He wasn't endeavoring to make a predictable salary; he was endeavoring to learn. He was searching for work with something important to teach him.

His rich dad had drilled it into him: having near no experience with a ton was huge for any person who expected to get cash. That is the explanation Robert was endeavoring to learn, not just obtain. In light of everything, getting cash was what his assets would be for.

His sad dad couldn't understand. To his cerebrum, Robert's approach to acting was the specific opposite of what compelled people to act. He was an insightful, cunning, and proficient man with a PhD. His way of life had taught him that it was specialization, not a sweeping base of capacities and data, that provoked riches.

In the academic world, the higher up you go and the more you learn, the more modest your subject of study. Essentially, experts are by and large restless to invest huge energy in a single field, like strong wellbeing or pediatrics, when they graduate.

For specific people, such rehearsing could give off the impression of being genuine. It didn't help lamentable dad, in any case, whose PhD never did a great deal to help his pay. Rich Dad, on the other hand, had a wide base of data, yet he never finished the eighth grade.

That is the explanation for how he enabled energetic Robert and Mike to focus on a whole host of different parts of his business space. Over an extended period of time, they worked in bistros and improvement, bargains and displays, records, and reservations.

The guide wasn't toward finding one single field they could happily seize the opportunity to spend their callings in; it was to outfit them with the extent of capacities and data essential for creating abundance. That is the explanation for the sixth and last model: don't just endeavor to procure; endeavoring to learn is extensively more critical.

Final summary

So it's as simple as that. We've shown up toward the end, covering the six head models from this example from two fathers. Remember, it was this very direction that laid the groundwork for monetary progress—an all-out resource of a normal 100,000,000 bucks.nDoes that have your attention again? Incredible—then it's the best open door for a fast recap. Model number one was that the well-off didn't have to work for cash. If you essentially stay in your useless everyday presence as far back as you can recall, it will propel someone, but it won't be you; it's your administrator, whose wallet you'll genuinely be stuffing. So what's the other choice? That enables us to outline two. Show yourself reserves, recognize verifiable assets, and put assets into them. Do this by following the directions from the third model: keep your typical regular work, limit your expenses, and moreover, have your business as an untimely idea to acquire cash for you.

Rule number four was: know fundamentally all that there is to know about the cost structure, since that is what rich people do, and they're prepared to consequently stick to their money. The fifth choice is that getting cash takes chutzpah, yet by accepting you have it, you can benefit from life's possibilities and "come up with" cash in essentially any situation.

To wrap things up, rule number six is: work to learn,